Y0-DOM-536

|| भेकराजः मण्डूकः ||

प्रकाशनम् – संस्कृतभारती, USA

लेखिका - विद्या रामनाथन् चित्ररचयित्री - अस्मिता रङ्गनाथन्

A Frog named Bhēkarājaḥ

Publisher – Samskrita Bharati, USA

Author – Vidya Ramanathan Illustratior – Asmita Ranganathan

Bi-lingual (English and संस्कृतम्) संस्कृतम् in Dual script – (Roman and देवनागरी)

www.samskritabharatiusa.org

email: info@samskritabharatiusa.org

मम नाम भेकराजः । अहं मण्डूकः ।

एषा मम कथा ।

mama nāma bhēkarājaḥ | ahaṁ maṇḍūkaḥ | ēṣā mama kathā |

My name is Bhēkarājaḥ. I am a frog.
This is my story.

भोः अम्ब ! भोः तात ! भोः अग्रजे !

भोः अनुज ! भोः मित्र !

सर्वे शृण्वन्तु ।

bhōḥ amba ! bhōḥ tāta ! bhōḥ agrajē ! bhōḥ anuja ! bhōḥ mitra ! sarvē śṛṇvantu |

Hi, there! Mom! Dad! Bro! Sis! Hey buddy! Listen!

Frog Bhēkarājaḥ is playing in a pond. His friends are with him. They leap and they play.

किञ्चन तडागम् । भेकराजः मण्डूकः
मण्डूकगणेन सह
प्लवमानः क्रीडति ।

kiñcana taḍāgam | bhēkarājaḥ maṇḍūkaḥ
maṇḍūkagaṇēna saha plavamānaḥ krīḍati |

Friend Snake says, “May I play, too?” Frog Bhēkarājaḥ says, “I leap! You slither! Can't play!”

मित्रं सर्पः वदति

अहम् अपि क्रीडामि । इति ।

भेकराजः वदति अहं प्लवे ।

भवान् तु

सरति । मास्तु ।

इति ।

mitraṁ sarpaḥ vadati aham api krīḍāmi | iti |

bhēkarājaḥ vadati ahaṁ plavē | bhavān tu sarati |

māstu | iti |

Friend Horse says, “May I play, too?” Frog Bhēkarājaḥ says, “I leap! You run! Can't play!”

मित्रम् अश्वः वदति

अहम् अपि क्रीडामि ।

इति ।

भेकराजः वदति

अहं प्लवे । भवान् तु धावति ।

मास्तु । इति ।

mitram aśvaḥ vadati aham api krīḍāmi iti | bhēkarājaḥ vadati ahaṁ plavē | bhavān tu dhāvati | māstu | iti |

Friend Cow says, “May I play, too?” Frog Bhēkarājaḥ says, “I leap! You graze! Can't play!”

मित्रं धेनुः वदति
अहम् अपि क्रीडामि ।
इति ।

भेकराजः वदति
अहं प्लवे । भवती तु चरति ।
मास्तु । इति ।

mitraṁ dhēnuḥ vadati aham api krīḍāmi | iti | bhēkarājaḥ vadati ahaṁ plavē | bhavatī tu carati | māstu | iti |

Friend Fish says, "May I play, too?" Frog Bhēkarājaḥ says, "I leap! You swim! Can't play!"

मित्रं मत्स्यः वदति

अहम् अपि क्रीडामि ।

इति ।

भेकराजः वदति

अहं प्लवे । भवान् तु तरति ।

मास्तु । इति ।

mitraṁ matsyaḥ vadati aham api krīḍāmi iti | bhēkarājaḥ vadati ahaṁ plavē | bhavān tu tarati | māstu | iti |

Friend Bee says, “May I play, too?” Frog Bhēkarājaḥ says, “I leap! You buzz! Can't play!”

मित्रं भ्रमरः वदति

अहम् अपि क्रीडामि ।

इति ।

भेकराजः वदति

अहं प्लवे । भवान् तु भ्रमति ।

मास्तु । इति ।

mitraṁ bhramaraḥ vadati aham api krīḍāmi iti | bhēkarājaḥ vadati ahaṁ plavē | bhavān tu bhramati | māstu | iti |

Friend Monkey says, “May I play, too?” Frog Bhēkarājaḥ says, “I leap! You swing! Can't play!”

मित्रं वानरः वदति

अहम् अपि क्रीडामि ।

इति ।

भेकराजः वदति

अहं प्लवे । भवान् तु लङ्घते ।

मास्तु । इति ।

mitraṁ vānaraḥ vadati aham api krīḍāmi iti | bhēkarājaḥ vadati ahaṁ plavē | bhavān tu laṅghatē | māstu | iti |

Brother Bhēkakumāraḥ says, "May I play, too?" Frog Bhēkarājaḥ says, "I leap! You … Oh! You leap too! Come along. Friends! Come along. Let us all play together! "

अनुजः भेककुमारः वदति
अहम् अपि क्रीडामि । इति ।

भेकराजः वदति अहं प्लवे । भवान् तु ... हा ! भवान् अपि प्लवते । आयातु । भो! मित्राणि आयान्तु । क्रीडामः। इति।

anujaḥ bhēkakumāraḥ vadati aham api krīḍāmi iti |

bhēkarājaḥ vadati ahaṁ plavē | bhavān tu ... | hā ! bhavān api plavatē | āyātu | bhō ! mitrāṇi āyāntu | krīḍāmaḥ iti |

Later, frog Bhēkarājaḥ, brother Bhēkakumāraḥ, the other frogs, and all the friends play together.

अनन्तरं भेकराजः मण्डूकः

अनुजः भेककुमारः

मण्डूकगणः

अन्यानि मित्राणि च

क्रीडन्ति ।

anantaraṁ bhēkarājaḥ maṇḍūkaḥ anujaḥ bhēkakumāraḥ
maṇḍūkagaṇaḥ anyāni mitrāṇi ca krīḍanti |

Snake slithers.

सर्पः सरति ।

sarpaḥ sarati |

Horse runs

अश्वः धावति ।

aśvaḥ dhāvati |

Cow grazes

धेनुः चरति ।

dhēnuḥ carati |

Fish swims.

मत्स्यः तरति ।

matsyaḥ tarati |

Bee buzzes.

भ्रमरः भ्रमति ।

bhramaraḥ bhramati |

Monkey swings.

वानरः लङ्घते ।

vānaraḥ laṅghatē |

Frog leaps.

मण्डूकः प्लवते ।

maṇḍūkaḥ plavatē |

Animals move so.

एवं मृगाः चलन्ति ।

ēvaṁ mr̥gāḥ calanti |

प्लवमानस्य मण्डूकस्य चलनं

मण्डूकप्लुतिः इति उच्यते ।

plavamānasya maṇḍūkasya calanaṁ **maṇḍūkaplutiḥ** iti ucyatē |

To leap like a frog is to leapfrog.

॥ भेके मण्डूकवर्षाभूशालूरप्लवदर्दुराः ॥

॥ वारिवर्गः ॥ ॥ अमरकोषः ॥

|| bhēkē maṇḍūkavarṣābhūśālūraplavadardurāḥ ||

|| vārivargaḥ || || amarakōṣaḥ ||

The various names for a frog are bhēkaḥ, maṇḍūkaḥ, varṣābhūḥ, śālūraḥ, plavaḥ and darduraḥ.

padasaṅgrahaḥ	पदसङ्ग्रहः	Vocabulary

taḍāgam	तडागम्	pond		krīḍati	क्रीडति	(he) plays
mitram	मित्रम्	friend		krīḍanti	क्रीडन्ति	(they) play
mitrāṇi	मित्राणि	friends		krīḍāmi	क्रीडामि	(I) play
aham	अहम्	I		krīḍāmaḥ	क्रीडामः	(we) play
bhavān	भवान्	you (boy)		plavatē	प्लवते	(he) leaps
bhavatī	भवती	you (girl)		plavē	प्लवे	(I) leap
maṇḍūkaḥ	मण्डूकः	frog		māstu	मास्तु	Won't do!
maṇḍūkasya	मण्डूकस्य	frog's		vadati	वदति	(he) says
Iti	इति	thus / so		vadanti	वदन्ति	(they) say
Api	अपि	also		vadāmi	वदामि	(I) say
nāma	नाम	name		vadāmaḥ	वदामः	(we) say
ambā	अम्बा	mother		śṛṇōtu	शृणोतु	please listen
tātaḥ	तातः	father		śṛṇvantu	शृण्वन्तु	(all) please listen
agrajā	अग्रजा	(older) sister		calati	चलति	(it) moves
anujaḥ	अनुजः	(younger) brother		calanti	चलन्ति	(they) move
Tu	तु	but		āyātu	आयातु	please come
ēvam	एवम्	in this manner		āyāntu	आयान्तु	(all) please come

A Few Words from the Author

About the format - The objective is to have the child enjoy reading the story in Samskritam.

Colors, size and placement of the various texts maximize the focus on Samskritam and the Devanagari script.

The English rendering and the Roman script are meant to aid this process.

The book can be read by the child, or, a parent can read it out to the child.

I thank Avinash Varna for initial editorial guidance and encouragement. Suggestions and comments are welcome.

I thank Asmita Ranganathan for the absolutely wonderful illustrations that have added a new dimension to the story and brought it alive. Our hero, the frog with a prominent birthmark on his cheek, is indeed adorable. I thank all those who have played minor and major roles in the fruition of this book.

I thank those who placed their trust in me, and sponsored the publication of this book.
Well-wishers interested in sponsoring future publications, please contact info@samskritabharatiusa.org

All proceeds from this book will go towards the publication of more books for children, by various authors, on various topics - all to captivate the young hearts and imagination of our children.

CPSIA information can be obtained
at www.ICGtesting.com
Printed in the USA
LVIC06n0743011213
363299LV00008B/23
9780989594813